T0374025

A Walk through End Times Bible Prophecy

Mark May

WestBow Press books may be ordered through booksellers or by contacting:

WestBow Press
A Division of Thomas Nelson & Zondervan
1663 Liberty Drive
Bloomington, IN 47403
www.westbowpress.com
1 (866) 928-1240

ISBN: 978-1-4908-3458-0 (sc)
ISBN: 978-1-4908-3457-3 (e)

Library of Congress Control Number: 2014908978

Printed in the United States of America.

WestBow Press rev. date: 06/17/2014

WestBow
PRESS
A DIVISION OF THOMAS NELSON
& ZONDERVAN

PREFACE

Not long ago my brother and I were painting a friend's house. As a teenager my brother had accepted Jesus as his Lord but, over the years he has drifted away from God. As we talked, our conversation eventually turned to a discussion about religion. It was then that he commented that he didn't understand why God doesn't communicate directly to us anymore, and why he leaves so much up to faith! For a moment I couldn't respond, a thousand different answers to his question ran through my mind.

I thought about using the Israelites who followed Moses out of Egypt as an example. They got to see the power of God firsthand. First through the plagues that God brought to free them from captivity. Then by the whirl wind of dust in the day, and fire by night that he used to protect and lead them. The parting of the Red Sea as Pharos army pursued them. His care for them in the wilderness when he gave them manna and quail to eat and water to drink . Yet despite all the marvelous things that God did to prove his presence and love for his people, many chose to forsake him as soon as Moses left them to receive the 10 commandments.

Ultimately I answered my brother by explaining that God does communicate directly to us. He's done it by writing his words in a book known as the holy bible. That book took over 1,800 years for him to write. In it he explains how we should live our lives and treat those around us. He warns us about the traps that Satan will use to try and deceive us, and what the consequences of following those are. He also tells us what we need to do to receive his grace. And it is there that he also reveals what his plans for mankind and this world are.

Some think that if there is a God he doesn't care about us, or that he is just sitting idly by watching what happens in the world. I can assure you that he cares very much, and knows exactly what is going on. God has a definite plan and purpose for this world. If we want to know what that plan is and what God has to say, we need to read his book. One doesn't have to be a scholar, they just need to read and let God's words speak for themselves.

Sadly, there are many who choose not to read the words God has given to us. By doing so they miss the message of love and hope that he has for them. The love of a God who was willing to die on a cross to pay the price of our sins. The hope that he will indeed someday return as he tells us he will and establish a new heaven and earth. One where those who do follow him will live and dwell for all eternity.

Does God communicate with us? Yes he does. It's up to us though to hear and answer him. In the following pages we will explore several bible passages to discover what God's plan for his people and this world which he created are. It is my hope that as we do so, you will begin to truly understand the love that God has for us, and his desire that we spend eternity in his presence.

A Brief Explanation of
CHRISTIAN MILLENIAL POSITIONS

For many Christians the study of the future is about the promised return of Jesus Christ. When that occurs it will be to defeat Satan and his followers, and establish Gods eternal kingdom here on earth. Although no one knows for certain when that day will come, Jesus did say that several things had to happen before he does return (Matthew 24). There are numerous prophecies God gave in which he details the events that are to happen before and at the time of his return. The study of these prophesies is known as *"eschatology"* from the Greek word *"eschatos"* meaning *"last"*. Eschatology is *"a study of last things"* or, *"Doctrine of the future"*.

Throughout the course of history, many have studied the prophetic passages God has given to try and understand when and how the events he foretold will occur. Many different views have arisen on both the timing of Christ's return, and whether it is to occur in one or two parts. **Early church's believed that Jesus followers would be caught up in the air (1 Thess. 4:17), followed by judgment of unbelievers on earth, and a millennium period of grace**. Others believed **that Christ's return would not occur until either the middle (amillennial), or end (postmillennial) of the millennium period.**

The concept of Christ's return in two phases, **rapture of the church, followed by his physical return(2nd coming), with a tribulation period (7 years),** did not become popular until the 17th century. This belief known as Dispensationalisim was popularized by the English Brethren Church leader, John Nelson Darby in 1827.

Despite these many differing opinions there are certain aspects of Christ's return that all evangelicals do agree on. It is important to take a look at those before we proceed on.

1. **Areas of Agreement among Christians:**

   A. The sudden, personal, visible return of Christ.

      Matt. 24, John 14: 3, Acts 1: 11, 1 Thess. 4: 16, Heb. 9:28, 2 Pet. 3: 10, Rev. 22: 20

   B. We should eagerly long for the return of Christ.

      Rev . 22: 20 "Amen. Come Lord Jesus!", Titus 2: 12&13, 1 Cor. 16: 22 | "Our Lord Come"

   C. We do not know when Christ will return.

      Matt. 24: 44: 25: 13, Mark 13: 32&33

   D. All Christians agree on the Final Results of Christs return.

      Judgment of unbelievers, final reward of believers, believers will live with Christ in a new heaven and new earth for all eternity. God the Father, Son and Holy Spirit will reign and will be worshiped in a never ending kingdom with no sorrow, sin or suffering.

2. **Signs that will Precede Christ's return:**

      Gospel to All Nations – Matt. 24: 14, Mark 13: 10
      Great Tribulation – Mark 13: 7&8, Matt. 24: 15-22, Luke 21: 20-24
      False Prophets, Signs and Wonders – Matt. 24: 23&24, Mark 13: 22
      Signs in Heaven – Mark 13: 24&25
      Coming of the Man of Sin - Thess. 2: 1-10
      Salvation of Israel – Rom. 11: 25-26

We currently live in what is commonly understood by the Christian Church as *"The Church Age"*. This is the period after Jesus ascension into heaven when he commanded his disciples to *"go into the world and teach the nations about him"* (Matthew 28: 18-20). The end of this period will occur when Jesus physically returns to earth to live and dwell among us (Acts 1: 10 & 11).

Revelation 20 describes a period of a thousand years known as the **millennium,** that will take place when the Church Age ends. Throughout the history of the church, three prominent positions have arisen on the time and nature of the millennium. We will also look at these in brief but again, there are certain events that occur after the millennium which all evangelicals generally agree on.

1. At the end of the Millennium there will be a final judgment where Jesus tells us that all will finally acknowledge him as Lord.

2. Those that chose to reject him as Lord in life will be cast into the lake of fire to be tormented for all eternity.

3. Those that acknowledge Jesus as Lord in life will enter eternity and live with him in the New Heaven and Earth that is described in Revelation 21.

With these basic understandings we will now take a brief look at each of the 3 prominent millennial positions:

Pre Millennialism

A term that includes a variety of views that have in common, the belief that Christ will return before the Millennium. **Pre Millennialists believe that the return of Christ will occur in two stages**. In the first event known as the **Rapture**, (1 Thessalonians 4: 15-17) the saved are to be <u>caught up</u> <u>to meet Jesus in the air</u>. The **Second Coming** occurs when Christ <u>physically returns to earth</u> with the heavenly host to battle Satan and his followers. The timing between these two events differs, depending on position.

Dispensationalists favor the Pre Millennial position because it allows for a clear distinction between The Church and Israel to be maintained. The Church will be removed (raptured) before a widespread conversion of the Jewish people that occurs during the tribulation period **(Rev. 7: 4).** This will allow for the Old Testament prophesies of God's future blessings to Israel to be fulfilled among the Jewish people themselves.

While all Dispensationalists are Pre Millennialist, they may differ on their belief of when the rapture and second coming will take place. The three prominent Pre Millennial views on the timing of these events are given below.

Pre Tribulation

The pre tribulation position believes that the **rapture** will occur at the start of a **seven year tribulation period**. The **second coming** will occur at the end of this tribulation period. Pre-tribulationists describe the rapture as Jesus coming <u>for</u> the church, and the second coming as Jesus coming <u>with</u> the church. The seven year period of tribulation will be a time of the outpouring of **God's wrath** on the earth. Christians would not have to endure the tribulation since they will be raptured at its beginning.

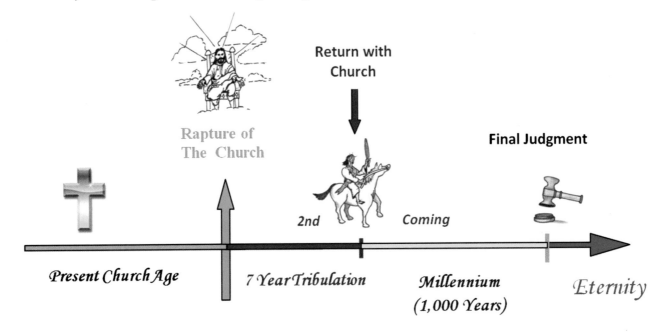

Pre Tribulation Time Line

Mid Tribulation

The mid tribulation position believes that the **rapture** will occur at some point in the middle of the **tribulation period, also described as Daniel's 70ᵗʰ week (Dan. 9: 27).** Here, the tribulation is divided into two periods of 3 ½ years each. Mid Tribulationists believe that the saints will go through the first period (beginning of travail) and be raptured into heaven before the severe outpouring of God's wrath in the second half of the Tribulation. Mid Tribulationists appeal to **Daniel 7: 25** which says the saints will be given over to tribulation for *"time, times, and half a time."*

interpreted to mean 3 ½ years. At the halfway point of the tribulation, the Antichrist will commit the **"abomination of desolation" (Dan. 11: 31)** by desecrating the temple in Jerusalem and provoking God's anger.

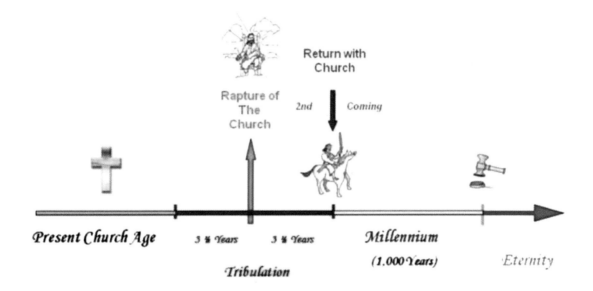

Mid Tribulation Time Line

Post Tribulation

The post tribulation position places the **rapture** at the end of the tribulation period. Post tribulation proponents define the tribulation period in a generic sense as the entire present age, or in a specific sense of a period of time preceding the **second coming** of Christ. The emphasis in this view is that the church will undergo the Tribulation but, that it will be spared the wrath of God. The passages of **Mathew 24: 29-31** are cited as the foundational scripture for this view. Post tribulationists perceive the rapture as occurring simultaneously with the second coming of Christ. When Jesus returns believers will meet him in the air and immediately accompany him as he returns to the earth.

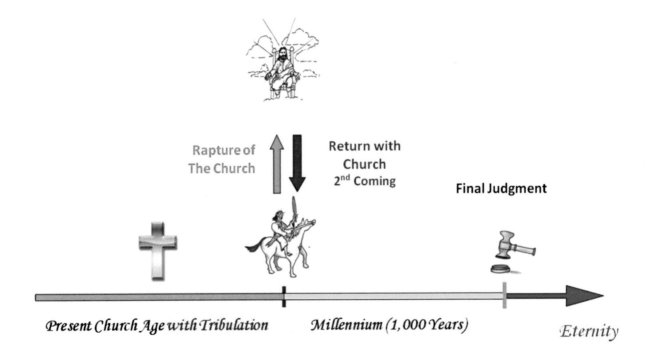

Post Tribulation Time Line

A Millennialism

This view believes that **"thousand years"** is a figure of speech for a long period of time in which God's purposes will be accomplished. This view allows for **Revelation 20: 1-10** to be interpreted as the present church age. In this age Satan's influence over the world has been greatly reduced, allowing the gospel to be preached to all the world. Christ's reign is not bodily on earth, but instead a heavenly reign as spoken in **Matt. 28: 18** *"All power is given unto me in heaven and in earth."*

The A Millennialist believe that the binding of Satan described in Revelation 20: 1 - 3 occurred during Jesus earthly ministry. In **Matt. 12: 29** Jesus spoke of binding the strong man in order that he (Jesus) may plunder his house. This binding was for the specific purpose *"that he should deceive the nations no more (vs.3)."*

AMillenialist believe the church age will continue until the time of Christ return. The bodies of believers will then rise to meet their spirit and enter the full enjoyment of heaven forever (vs.5). Unbelievers will be raised to stand before the judgment seat of Christ. Believers will also stand at the judgment seat however, it will be to determine degrees of reward in heaven.

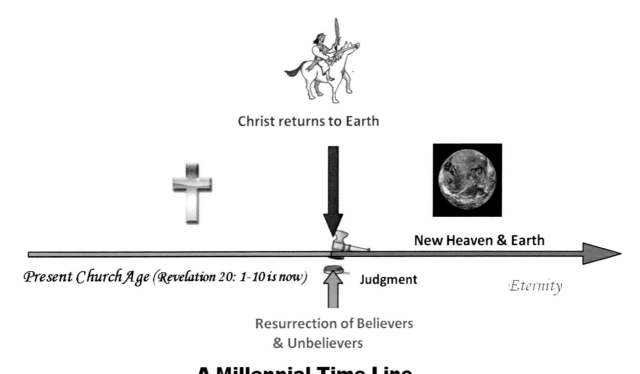

Christ returns to Earth

New Heaven & Earth

Present Church Age (Revelation 20: 1-10 is now)   Judgment   *Eternity*

Resurrection of Believers
& Unbelievers

A Millennial Time Line
(No Future Millennium)

Post Millennialism

The view that Christ will return to the earth after the millennium. In this view the millennium is an age of peace and righteousness on earth brought about by the progress of the gospel and the growth of the church. This is based on the words of Jesus in the great commission **Matt. 28: 18 -20** *"All power is given unto me in heaven and earth. Go ye therefore, and teach all nations, baptizing them in the name of the Father, and of the Son, and of the Holy Ghost. Teaching them to observe all things whatsoever I have commanded you: and lo, I am with you always,* <u>*even unto the end of the world.*</u>*"* Thus if Jesus has all authority, the gospel will go forward and the world will get better and better.

The parables of **Matthew 13: 31 - 32, & 33** are also used to support the position that through the gradual growth of the kingdom, the whole earth will be filled with its influence.

It must be noted that the Post Millennial view of the millennium differs significantly from that of the Pre Millennialist. While the Pre Millennialists talk about a renewed earth with Jesus Christ physically present and reigning as King, together with glorified believers in resurrected bodies, Post Millennialists are talking about an earth with many Christians influencing society. A renewed earth and glorified saints do not occur until after Christ returns to inaugurate the eternal state.

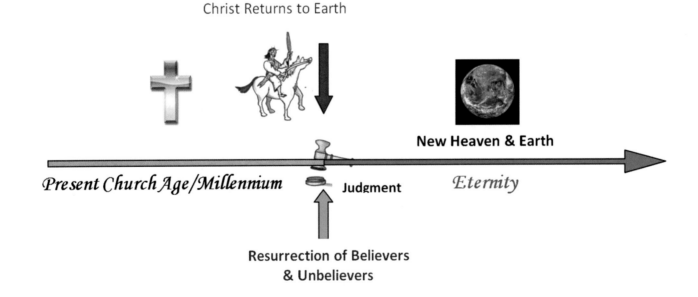

PostMillennial Time Line

Understanding The Prophetic Symbols of the Bible

One of my favorite passages of the bible is found in **Isaiah 46: 9 & 10**. At the time it was written, the Jewish nation had allowed the teachings from other false religions to creep into their society. After reminding them that the gods of these religions had no real power, God commands his people saying, *"Remember the former things of old for I am God and there is none else: I am God and there is none like me. Declaring the end from the beginning, and from ancient times the things that are not yet done, saying: My counsel shall stand and I will do all my pleasure:"*

In this statement God voids those other false religions by reminding his people that he alone is the only true God. He affirms this by reminding them that only he knows the end of time from the beginning, and it is he that reveals those events yet to come to us. None of their idols made of gold, silver or stone had the ablility to do this.

It would follow then that some will ask, when and how have these declarations been made? Well, first through the visions God gave to his prophets. Second, through the teachings and statements he himself made during his ministry here on earth. Both the visions and his statements have all been meticulously recorded for us in the Holy Scriptures.

So then why do so many people come to differing opinions on their meaning when they read them? It would be easy to say that our human nature is to blame. We often read or hear, only what we want to read or hear. Since every true believer longs for Christ's return, they sometimes look at the problems in the world around them and try to make a prophesy fit those situations. It's an easy thing to do since we live in a world where sin abounds and there is so much of it. God has told us though that we will always face problems. He also tells us to take heart and not get discouraged because *he has overcome this world*.

The answer to correctly understanding Gods prophesy and teachings is actually simpler than people might expect. First, as one begins to read them it becomes apparent that they are filled with metaphors and allegorical symbols. We'll discuss why God does this in a minute but, it goes without saying that if we want to correctly understand the meaning of a particular prophesy, we need to understand the meaning of the symbols and metaphors God uses in it.

How do we do this? It's really not hard, in fact God tells us what each symbol means (Revelation 1:20). Because the meanings are consistent throughout the bible, they can be applied to every prophecy. The table below lists just a few of the more common symbols and their interpretations.

PROPHETIC SYMBOLS OF THE BIBLE

WATERS / RIVERS: Represent Peoples/Nations (Rev. 17: 5)

MOUNTAINS &HEADS: Represent Kingdoms (Rev. 17: 9)

WOMAN: Represents a Spiritual Entity with a literal Kingdom & Capital (Rev. 12: 17)

BEAST: Represents Empires led by Kings/Always represents a group of people that follow a false religion & its leader (horn).

EMPIRES: Represent a collective group of many people

HORNS: Represent Rulers or Kings

FISH: Represents followers

PROPHETIC SYMBOLS OF THE BIBLE
(Continued)

A STONE or ROCK: Represents the Messiah (Dan. 2)

STARS: Represent Angels

DRAGON: Represents Satan

**TREES & BIRDS: With the exception of the Olive Tree,
        Represent Fallen Angels (Ezek. 31: 3&4)**

Some of you are now undoubtedly wondering, why God choose to use these symbols and metaphors when he gave us his prophecy? Why didn't he just say what he wanted to say in a clear and simple manner?

For that answer let's look at a lesson the Lord taught to his disciples in Mark Chapter 4.

MARK 4

1. *And he (Jesus) began again to teach by the sea side: and there was gathered unto him a great multitude, so that he entered into a ship, and sat in the sea: and the whole multitude was by the sea on the land.*

2. *And he taught them many things by parables……..*

   (10) And when he was alone, they that were about him with the twelve asked of him the parable.

   (11) And he said unto them, Unto you it is given to know the mystery of the kingdom of God; but unto them that are without , all these things are done in parables:

(12) That seeing they may see, and not perceive; and hearing they may hear, and not understand; least at any time they should be converted, and their sins should be forgiven them.

Is God saying that he doesn't want to forgive some people so that they can not enjoy eternal life? Not at all, remember the great commission that Jesus later gave his disciples? He commanded them to **go into all the world and teach and make disciples**. His desire is not that any should be lost, but that all should be saved.

Here Jesus is just explaining for his disciples and us a painful truth. That is that no matter how clearly you tell some people, they will never hear what you want them to hear. Jesus knew that there were many people in the crowd who where only there to see this new prophet that everyone was talking about. They are the ones who lack true faith **(Hebrews 4: 2&3)**. They didn't care so much what he was telling them, they were only there for the show. Therefore, Jesus speaks in parables that only his true followers will understand while the rest, those that don't care can say they came and heard him. Jesus knows that those who want to understand the truth are the ones that will come to him for the real meaning.

Lastly, we need to understand the dual nature of prophecy. For the person who was given the vision it may have an immediate meaning, yet hold another meaning entirely for us who later read it. Take for example a prophesy you may already be familiar with from Jeremiah 23 verses 5 & 6.

Jeremiah 23:

5. *Behold, the days come saith the Lord, that I will raise unto David a righteous Branch, and a King shall reign and prosper, and shall execute judgment and justice in the earth.* **6.** *In his days Judah shall be saved, and Israel shall dwell safely, and this is his name whereby he shall be called, THE LORD OUR RIGHTEOUSNESS.*

Jeremiah understood this was a promise to the Jews that the Messiah would come from the line of David. While the Jews still anxiously await the fulfillment of this prophecy, Christians understand that Jesus fulfilled that part of the promise. The first time he came to earth as our savior. The second time he will return as the Messiah. Then this prophecy will be complete. Thus, one meaning for Jeremiah and the Jews, a different meaning for us.

Johns Vision

Now that we understand a little bit about how God uses allegory & metaphors, let's look at the prophetic vision of John in Revelation 17. It is a prophecy that explains who will be in political control of the nations of the Middle Eastern region at the time Jesus does return. As you read you will notice that I have highlighted the allegorical symbols that are given, along with the explanations of their meanings.

<u>Revelation 17</u>

1. *And there came one of the seven angels which had the seven vials, and talked with me saying unto me, Come hither, I will shew unto thee the judgment of* **the great whore** *that sitteth upon* **many waters:**

2. *With whom the kings of the earth have committed fornication and the inhabitants of the earth have been made drunk with the wine of her fornication.*

3. *So he carried me away in the spirit into the wilderness: and I saw a woman sit upon a* **scarlet colored beast, full of names of blasphemy, having** <u>**seven heads and ten horns.**</u>

4. *And the woman was arrayed in purple and scarlet colour, and* decked with gold and precious stones and pearls, having a golden cup *in her hand full of abominations and filthiness of her fornication:*

5. *And upon her forehead was a name written, MYSTERY, BABYLON THE GREAT , THE MOTHER OF HARLOTS AND ABOMINATIONS OF THE EARTH.*

6. *And I saw the woman drunken with the blood of the saints, and with the blood of the martyrs of Jesus: and when I saw her, I wondered with great admiration.*

7. *And the angel said unto me, Wherefore didst thou marvel? I will tell thee the mystery of the woman, and of the beast that carrieth her, which hath the seven heads and ten horns.*

8. ***The beast that thou sawest was, and is not; and shall ascend out of the bottomless pit, and go into perdition: and they that dwell on the earth shall wonder, whose***

names were not written in the book of life from the foundation of the world, when they behold the beast that was, and is not , and yet is.

9. *And here is the mind which hath wisdom. The seven heads are seven mountains, on which the woman sitteth.*

10. ***And there are seven kings:*** **five are fallen, and one is, and the other is not yet come; and when he cometh, he must continue a short space.**

11. **And the beast that was and is not, even he is the eighth, and is of the seven, and goeth into perdition.**

12. **And the ten horns which thou sawest are ten kings, which have received no kingdom as yet; but receive power as kings one hour with the beast.**

13. *These have one mind, and shall give their power and strength unto the beast.*

14. *These shall make war with the Lamb, and the Lamb shall overcome them: for he is Lord of lords, and King of kings: and they that are with him are called, and chosen, and faithful.*

15. **And he saith unto me, The waters which thou sawest, where the whore sitteth, are peoples and multitudes, and nations, and tongues.**

16. *And the ten horns which thou sawest upon the beast, these shall hate the whore, and shall make her desolate and naked, and shall eat her flesh, and burn her with fire.*

17. *For God hath put in their hearts to fulfill his will, and to agree , and give their kingdom unto the beast, until the words of God shall be fulfilled.*

18. **And the woman which thou sawest is that great city, which reigneth over the kings of the earth.**

In verse 18 we see that the **woman (great whore) represents the capital city of an evil empire (beast).** This empire represented by the beast will be made up of a large mixture of **diverse peoples** (vs. 15). The city (capital) will use its great wealth to control the empire (vs. 4&5). This empire will wage war against Gods people, or those who follow Jesus (vs. 6).

In his book <u>Gods War on Terror</u>, author Walid Shoebat goes into great detail explaining how Satan will unite these nations under a false religion. The false religion that he explains Satan will use to deceive the nations is the religion of Islam. The word Islam means submission, and it is this religion that is now spreading throughout much of the world. I would encourage you to read his book, if you haven't yet done so.

As we see, the beast has **seven heads and ten horns** (vs. 3). We're told **the seven heads are seven mountains (kingdoms/empires), each with a king (seven kings, vs. 10). The key to unlocking the meaning of these empires is found in verse 10 where the Angel tells John that *"five of these kings are fallen, and one is, and the other is not yet come."*** At the time John received his vision, five major kingdoms had ruled over the Middle Eastern region. The Egyptian Empire was the first, followed by the Assyrian Empire, the Babylonian Empire, the Persian Empire, and the Greek Empire.

The ruler of the Greek empire was Alexander. After his assassination, the empire was divided into four regions. Each of these, north, south, east and west was then given to one of Alexander's generals to rule over.

The Romans were in control of the Middle East at the time John lived and received his vision (*one is*). The western portion of Roman Empire fell to Germanic Barbarians in AD 476 . The eastern portion of the Roman Empire continued on with its capital in Constantinople (Turkey) until it fell to Muslim Turks in AD 1453. The Turkish Ottoman Empire (Islamic) became the seventh head (***other is not yet come***; *and when he cometh, he must continue a short space).* This empire lasted until March 23, 1924. Thus explaining how the beast <u>was, and is not </u>(vs. 11).

We are then told that the beast will become an eighth head (empire) <u>that is of the seventh</u>. This eighth empire must thus be a version of the seventh which we know was the Islamic Ottoman Empire. This new eighth empire made up of 10 nations (10 horns), is the one that the Anti Christ will lead against God and the saints during the end times. The woman (great whore) we are told is the capital city of this evil empire.

In December of 2010 a movement known as the Arab Spring began in the Middle East. It was sparked by young adults who had become frustrated with the struggling economies and poor job opportunities in their Arab countries. The name Arab Spring was given to it because of the hope that it would bring renewal to these nations. To date, revolutions in Tunisia, Egypt, Libya, and Yemen have resulted in new governments and leaders for these countries. As I write this, Syria has been in an extended civil war that is expected to soon result in the removal of President Assad. Several leaders from other Arab countries have also announced that they will step down from office when their current terms expire. Interesting that Jesus told us in Matthew 24 that one of the signs that would proceed his return would be *"wars and rumors of wars".* This is what is now occurring in the Arab world.

Originally it was hoped that the governments that emerged from these revolutions would bring democracy and equality to their nations. What has occurred though has been just the opposite. The vacuum that occurred as the original governments have fallen is being filled by fundamental Islamic leaders. These are promoted by political groups such as the Muslim Brotherhood. The Muslim Brotherhood is the political arm of an ultra conservative branch of Islam. The sole purpose of the Muslim Brotherhood is to introduce Sharia (Islamic)Law into these countries. The forming of the eighth empire described in Johns vision is taking place right before our eyes.

REVELATION 17
The Scarlet Women and 7 Headed Beast

7 Heads = 7 Empires		10 Horns = 10 Kings		
	1st = Egyptian Empire	1		
	2nd = Assyrian Empire	1		
Fallen	3rd = Babylonian Empire	1		
	4th = Persian Empire	1		North Seluce
	5th = Greek Empire	4	Alexander	South Piolem
Is (@ time of John's writing)	6th = Roman Empire *	1		West Cassander
Not Yet	7th = Turkish Ottoman Empire (Islamic) **	1		East Lysimachus
(vs. 11) Beast= Antichrist	8th = Resurgence of Ottoman (Islamic) Empire			

Notes :
• The western portion of the Roman Empire fell AD 476 when a barbarian named Odoacer deposed the last western Roman emperor, Romulus Augustulus. The eastern portion of the Roman Empire with its capital in Constantinople (Turkey) continued on until it fell to the Muslim Turks lead by Mohomet II in AD 1453.

** Mohomet II renamed Constantinople Istanbul and the Ottoman Empire lasted until March 23, 1924.

Nebuchadnezzar's Dream

Let's now turn our attention to the dream of King Nebuchadnezzar in Daniel 2. We know that Nebuchadnezzar was king of Babylon and ruled over the Middle Eastern region at the time of Daniel. We understand from the text that the king had a dream about a giant statue that was made of different metals. The king was so troubled by this dream that he called for his magicians, astrologers, sorcerer's and advisors (Chaldeans) to interpret the dream for him. After petition God, Daniel was the only one able tell the king what he had dreamed, and provide an interpretation for him.

Daniel 2

1. _And in the second year of the reign of Nebuchadnezzar Nebuchadnezzar dreamed dreams, wherewith his spirit was troubled, and his sleep brake from him._

2. _Then the king commanded to call the magicians, and the astrologers, and the sorcerer's, and the Chaldeans, for to shew the king his dreams. So they came and stood before the king._

3. _And the king said unto them, I have dreamed a dream and my spirit was troubled to know the dream…………_

25. _The Arioch brought in Daniel before the king in haste, and said this unto him, I have found a man of the captives of Judah, that will make known unto the king the interpretation…………_

31. **_Thou, O king, sawest, and behold a great image. This great image, whose brightness was excellent, stood before thee, and the form thereof was terrible._**

32. _This images head was of fine gold,_ **_his breast and his arms of silver,_** _his belly and his thighs of brass,_

33. _His legs of iron,_ **_his feet part of iron and part of clay._**

34. _hou sawest till that a_ **_stone was cut out without hands,_** _which smote the image upon his feet that were of iron and clay, and brake them to pieces._

35. _Then was the iron, the clay, the brass, the silver, and the gold broken to pieces together, and_

*became like the chaff of the summer threshing floors; and the wind carried them away, that no place was found for them: and the **stone** that smote the image became a **great mountain**, and <u>filled the</u> <u>whole earth.</u>*

36. <u>*This is the dream; and we will tell the interpretation thereof before the king.*</u>

37. *Thou, O king, art a king of kings: for the God of heaven hath given thee a kingdom, power, and strength, and glory.*

38. *And wheresoever the children of men dwell, the beasts of the field and the fowls of the heaven hath he given into thine hand, and hath made thee ruler over them all.* **Thou art this head of gold.**

39. *And after thee shall arise another kingdom inferior to thee, and another third kingdom of brass, <u>which shall bear rule over all the earth.</u>*

40. *And the fourth kingdom shall be strong as iron: forasmuch as iron breaketh in pieces and subdueth all things: and as iron that breaketh all these, shall it break in pieces and bruise.*

41. *And whereas thou sawest **the feet and toes, part of potters clay, and part of iron, the kingdom shall be divided; but there shall be in it of the strength of the iron,** forasmuch as thou sawest the iron mixed with miry clay.*

42. **And as the toes of the feet were part of iron, and part of clay, so the kingdom shall be partly strong, and partly broken.**

43. **And whereas thou sawest iron mixed with miry clay, they shall mingle themselves with the seed of men: but they shall not cleave one to another, even as iron is not mixed with clay.**

44. **And in the days of these kings shall the God of heaven set up a kingdom, which shall never be destroyed: and the kingdom shall not be left to other people, but it shall break in pieces and consume all these kingdoms, and it shall stand for ever.**

45. **For as much as thou sawest that the stone was cut out of the mountain without hands, and that it brake in pieces the iron, the brass, the clay, the silver, and the gold; the great God hath make known to the king what shall come to pass hereafter: and the dream is certain, and the interpretation thereof sure.**

From Daniel's interpretation we understand that the image (statue) represents 4 different kingdoms. Each kingdom is represented by the different metals of the statue (vs. 32&33).

The head or first kingdom is made of gold. Daniel explains that this is the Babylonian Kingdom of Nebuchadnezzar (vs. 38). The second kingdom that will follow Nebuchadnezzar's

(Babylonia Empire) is represented by silver. This kingdom we are told in verse 39 will be inferior to the first. The Babylonian Empire eventually fell to the Medes and the Persians under the leadership of the Persian King Cyrus. Although the Persians were the more dominate of the two nations, their combination explains how this kingdom was considered inferior to the first.

The third kingdom is represented by brass. Verse 39 states that it will ***"bear rule over all the earth."*** It was the Grecian Empire that became this third kingdom. Led by Alexander the Great, the Grecians were able to expand their empire into Europe, the Middle East, and Northern Africa. This gave them control of most of the then known world or," ***all the earth***."

The fourth kingdom is described as being like iron (vs. 40). For years western scholars have interpreted this to mean the Roman Empire. We should remember though that God had given this dream to King Nebuchadnezzar who ruled over the Middle Eastern region (Iraq & greater Mesopotamia). The Romans were never able to control this region entirely. Although they made successful raids into the eastern region, each time they did they were quickly forced into retreat by the Parthinians. The battles between these two nations became known as the 100 Years War. The next empire that was able to successfully control the entire Middle Eastern region was the Turkish Ottoman Empire. As we have learned, it was this empire that crushed and defeated the remnant of the eastern Roman Empire in AD 1453. The fourth kingdom identified by legs of iron is not the Roman, but the Turkish Ottoman Empire. As we have also discussed, the dominate religion of this empire was Islam.

In the vision of John that we looked at in Revelation 17, we saw that the Anti Christ will lead a revived version of this Ottoman Empire (Islamic). In Nebuchadnezzar's dream we read that the legs of the image are made of iron, but the feet and toes are part iron and part clay (vs. 33). Like the 8th head on John's beast, the 10 toes made partly of Iron and partly of clay represent the same revival of the previous Ottoman Empire. Interestingly, the description of them (vs. 42 & 43) matches perfectly with the 10 horns of the beast described in Johns vision.

Over the centuries, scholars of the scriptures have tried to determine who these 10 nations are that will be led by the Anti Christ. Believing this fourth kingdom to be Roman, they have more recently pointed to the European Nations of the Common Market and European Union to make up these nations. Again, they have missed the point that these prophecies are all focused on the Middle East. Once we understand that it was the Turkish Ottoman Empire (Middle Eastern) that became the fourth kingdom, we will understand that these mysterious 10 nations must also come from that region.

The stone cut without hands (vs. 34) is none other than Jesus the Messiah. He will crush the feet of the image (Empire of the Anti Christ) and establish a new kingdom. This kingdom is to be greater than any of the previous kingdoms and will last forever (vs. 44).

Daniel concludes his interpretation by telling Nebuchadnezzar that it is God that has made known to him what shall come to pass, and that **the dream is certain,** and the interpretation thereof sure (vs. 45). Reaffirmation that Gods council surely stands, it will not change, and that he will do all his pleasure.

Stone cut without hands = *Messiah (Jesus)*

Vs. 34 Thou sawest till that a stone was cut out without hands, which smote the image upon his feet that were of iron and clay, and brake them to pieces.
35a. Then was the iron, the clay, the brass, the silver, and the gold broken to pieces *together*........*b.) and the stone that smote the image became a great mountain (kingdom), and filled the whole earth.*

Head of Gold = *Babylonian Empire*

Breast & Arms of Silver = *Medo Persian Empire*

Belly & Thighs of Brass = *Grecian Empire*

Legs of Iron = *Ottoman (Eastern Rome) Empire*

10 Toes = 10 Kings (see also 10 Horns of Rev. 17 & Dan. 7)

Feet Part Iron, Part Clay = *Revived Ottoman Empire (vs 43)*

DANIEL 2
Nebuchadnezzar's dream of
The Great Image

Daniel's Dream

Daniels dream like Nebuchadnezzar's, gives a vision of 4 future empires that are to rise and precede the return of Jesus the Messiah. As we will see, the empires described in his dream, match perfectly with those in Nebuchadnezzar's. They also correlate with those of the 7 headed beast that we looked at in Revelation 17. Remember, John received his visions some 700 years after Daniel and Nebuchadnezzar.

Daniel 7

1. *In the first year of Belshazzar king of Babylon Daniel had a dream and visions of his head upon his bed: then he wrote the dream, and told the sum of the matters.*

2. *Daniel spake and said, I saw in my vision by night, and behold, the four winds of the heaven strove upon the **great sea.***

3. *And **four great beasts** came up from the **sea,** diverse one from another.*

4. *The first was like a lion, and had eagle's wings: I beheld till the wings thereof were plucked, and it was lifted up from the earth, and made stand upon the feet as a man, and a man's heart was given to it.*

5. *And behold another beast, a second, like to a bear, and it raised up itself on one side, and it had **three ribs** in the mouth of it between the teeth of it: **And they said thus unto it**, Arise, devour much flesh.*

6. *After this I beheld, and lo another, like a leopard, which had upon the back of it four wings of a fowl; the beast had also four heads; and dominion was given to it.*

7. *After this I saw in the night visions, and behold **a fourth beast, dreadful and terrible, and strong exceedingly; and it had great iron teeth:** it devoured and brake in pieces, and stamped the residue with the feet of it: and it was diverse from al the beasts that were befo0re it; **and it had ten horns.***

8. *I considered the horns, and behold, there came up among them **another little horn, before***

whom there were three of the first horns plucked up by the roots: **and,** *behold, in this horn were eyes like the eyes of man, and a mouth speaking great things.*

9. *I beheld till the thrones were cast down, and the* <u>*Ancient of days*</u> *did sit, whose garment was white as snow, and the hair of his head like the pure wool: his throne was like the fiery flame, and his wheels as burning fire.*

10. *A fiery stream issued and came forth from before him: thousand thousands ministered unto him, and ten thousand times ten thousand stood before him: the judgment was set, and the books were opened.*

11. *I beheld then because of the voice of the great words which* **the horn** *spake: I beheld even till the beast was slain, and his body destroyed, and given to the burning flame.*

12. *As concerning the rest of the beasts, they had their dominion taken away: yet their lives were prolonged for a season and time.*

13. *I saw in the night visions, and behold, o***ne like the** <u>Son of man</u> **came with the clouds of heaven,** *and came to the Ancient of days, and they brought him near before him.*

14. *And there was given him dominion, and glory, and a kingdom, that all people, nations, and languages, should serve him: his dominion is an everlasting dominion, which shall not pass away, and his kingdom that which shall not be destroyed.*

15. *I Daniel was grieved in my spirit in the midst of my body, and the visions of my head troubled me.*

16. *I came near unto one of them that stood by, and asked him the truth of all this. So he told me, and made me know the interpretation of the things.*

17. **These great beasts, which are four, are four kings, which shall arise out of the earth.**

18. *But the saints of the most High shall take the kingdom, and posses the kingdom forever, even forever and ever.*

19. *Then I would know the truth of the fourth beast which was diverse from all the others, exceeding dreadful, whose teeth were of iron, and his nails of brass: which devoured, brake in pieces, and stamped the residue with his feet:*

20. *And the ten horns that were in his head, and of* *the other* **which came up, and before whom three fell;** *even of that horn that had eyes, and a mouth spake very great things, whose look was more stout than his fellow.*

21. *I beheld, and the same horn made war with the saints, and prevailed against them:*

22. *Until the Ancient of days came, and judgment was given to the saints of the most High: and the time came that the saints possessed the kingdom.*

23. *Thus he said, The fourth beast shall be the fourth kingdom upon earth, which shall be diverse form all kingdoms, and shall devour the whole earth, and shall tread it down, and break it in pieces.*

24. **And the ten horns out of this kingdom are ten kings that <u>shall</u> arise and another shall rise after them: and he shall be <u>diverse</u> from the first, and he shall subdue three kings.**

25. *And he shall speak great words against the most High and shall wear out the saints of the most High, and think to <u>change times and laws:</u> and they shall be given into his hand until a time and times and the dividing of time.*

26. <u>**But the judgment shall sit**</u>, *and they shall take away his dominion, to consume and to destroy it unto the end.*

27. **And the kingdom and dominion, and the greatness of the kingdom under the whole heaven shall be given to the people of the saints of the most High whose kingdom is an everlasting kingdom, and all dominion shall serve and obey him.**

28. *Hitherto is the end of the matter. As for me Daniel, **my cogitations much troubled me, and my countenance changed in me:** but I kept the matter in my heart*

Daniels dream begins (vs. 3) with **4 different (diverse) beasts (kings)** rising out of the **sea (peoples).** In verse 17 we read that these **great beasts are 4 kings.**

The first beast is described as being like **a lion with eagles wings** (vs. 4). Throughout scripture the nation of Babylon is referenced as a lion (Jeremiah 4:7: 51). The symbol of the lion also appears throughout much of the art and architecture associated with the Babylonian empire. This first beast is undoubtedly a reference to the Babylonian Empire.

The second beast is described as being like **a bear which rises on its side** with **3 ribs in its mouth** (vs. 5). As we have discussed, the Babylonian Empire fell to the Medo Persian Empire. Persia consists of modern day Iran, Media is modern day Kurdistan. At the time, Persia was the more dominate of the two nations. The Bear rising on one side symbolizes the resurgence of the Persian (Iran) portion of the empire.

There are several interpretations as to what the three ribs in the Bears mouth symbolize. Some identify them as symbols of Satan, the Anti Christ and the False Prophet. I doubt those to be accurate because as we will see, they are described with other symbols (4th beast, little horn) later in this vision. The ribs cannot be other nations because they too are the wrong symbols. They must then symbolize something else.

Recently Israel was involved in another military skirmish against the Palestinians in the Gaza Strip. This skirmish started because of a campaign begun by the Palestinians to indiscriminately launch rockets and bombs over the border into Israel. Israel has been involved in similar skirmishes with the Palestinians located in the West Bank, and southern Lebanon. Most if not all the rockets and bombs used by the Palestinians are believed to have been obtained from Iran.

The dominant political party of the Palestinians is named Hamas. This party is based on the principles of Islamic fundamentalism. Its stated purpose is to liberate Palestine from Israeli occupation and to establish an Islamic state in what is now Israel, the West Bank and Gaza Strip. Hamas receives both strong political and monetary support from Iran. Iran has already made public its desire to destroy the Jewish nation of Israel. It thus makes sense that the Palestinians in these 3 regions (ribs) would encourage and support Iran in any act of aggression against the Israeli nation.

The third beast is described as being like a leopard with 4 wings on its back and 4 heads (vs. 6). A leopard symbolizes the speed in which the Greeks led by Alexander the Great conquered the then known world. The 4 heads are the generals to whom the empire was divided after Alexander's assassination.

The fourth beast is described as being dreadful, terrible and strong with great iron teeth and 10 horns (vs. 7). Daniel goes on to describe **another little horn which rises from among the 10, knocking out 3 of the first horns (vs. 8). This horn is described as having eyes like a man and a mouth speaking great (blasphemous) things.**

The vision of the four beasts, especially the fourth, troubles Daniel so much that he asked for an interpretation of his dream (vs. 16). He is told that the 4th beast is the 4th kingdom on earth (vs. 23). The kingdom of this beast (king) will be diverse (different) from all the other kingdoms, devouring the whole earth and tearing it down.

The 10 horns of the beast are 10 kings which will rise up (vs. 20 & 24). An **11th king** that is different from the others will then rise up. This king is described as having eyes and a mouth that speak great things against God (vs. 25). He will make war against the saints (vs. 21) and wear them out (vs. 25). By now you should realize that this king is none other than the Anti Christ, Satan himself.

At this point Jesus will return (vs. 22) and defeat the beast (Satan). He will establish an everlasting kingdom (vs. 27) in which his saints will dwell with him.

Even though it is explained to Daniel that God will prevail and the 4th beast will be defeated, the vision of it and the Anti Christ troubled Daniel greatly. He explains that his thoughts continued to trouble him and his countenance changed (vs. 28). While we can be reassured that God will ultimately be victorious, the end times are still going to be frightening. Joel 3 describes those days as days in which all the inhabitants of the world will tremble. In the days that lead up to the last great battle, Satan will use many tricks to try and deceive mankind into following him. Many will fall for his tricks and chose the path to destruction. Those saints that elect to follow Jesus will suffer great persecution before Gods intervention. Daniel was given a vision of this period, and was frightened by the power the beast was able to use over the unsaved.

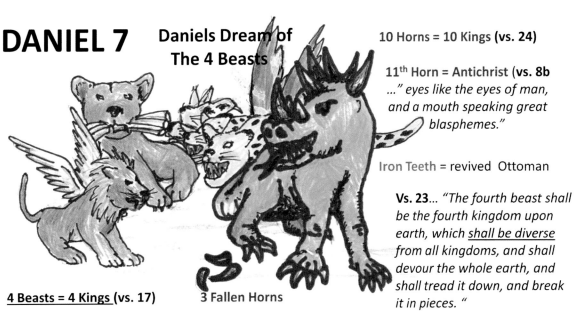

DANIEL 7 Daniels Dream of The 4 Beasts

10 Horns = 10 Kings (vs. 24)

11th Horn = Antichrist (vs. 8b …" *eyes like the eyes of man, and a mouth speaking great blasphemes."*

Iron Teeth = revived Ottoman

Vs. 23… *"The fourth beast shall be the fourth kingdom upon earth, which shall be diverse from all kingdoms, and shall devour the whole earth, and shall tread it down, and break it in pieces. "*

4 Beasts = 4 Kings (vs. 17)   3 Fallen Horns

1st Lion = Nebuchadnezzar (Babylonian)
2nd Bear = Medo Persian (Iran rises)
3rd 4 Headed Leopard = Alexander (Grecian)
4th Dreadful, Terrible, Strong = Anti Christ (Revived Islamic Ottoman)
vs.'s 8 & 11 The 4th Beast shall be destroyed by The Ancient of Days, and thrown into burning fire.

The Seal, Trumpet and Bowel Judgments of the Book of REVELATION

Perhaps nowhere else in the Bible does God reveal more of those events that will occur during the end times, than in the book of Revelation. Here are described for us are both the heavenly and earthly events that are to lead up to his return to earth. The purpose as we know will be for the final battle against the armies of Satan at the place known as Armageddon. The last book in the bible in which these events are revealed is also known to many as the Apocalypse. The prophetic visions it contains where given to the Apostle John at the end of his life while he was in exile on the isle of Patmos. It is the only book in the bible that promises to give readers a special blessing for keeping the things written in it (Rev. 1: 3), and pronounces a curse on those who try to tamper with its contents (Rev. 22: 18, 19).

Many have read this book and tried to unlock the meaning of the visions that John describes in it. There have been countless books written by those who believe they have found and clearly understand them. While it is not my intent to challenge any of these, I believe important points have been missed or overlooked in some of them. What follows is an attempt to fill in some of those blanks for us!

As we have now seen and discussed, God has <u>not</u> hidden anything from us. In fact we have seen how every prophecy contains a key (Rev. 17: 10) that will help us unlock and understand its true meaning. These keys also serve to tie the visions of <u>all</u> the biblical prophets together, so that their prophecies fit together like the pieces of a puzzle. As these pieces fit together we begin to see for ourselves what God's ultimate plan for the future is.

In the book of Revelation God gives John a vision in which he is shown the judgments that will be poured out on a sinful and rebellious world during the last days. The actions and events of these judgments begin by the breaking of the seven seals, the blowing of seven trumpets, and the pouring out of the seven bowels or vials. For the casual reader it is easy to become confused as they read the passages that detail these events. Some appear to occur in heaven, some on earth. Some seem to be muddled together with each other so that It can be easy to lose track of what, when, and where, everything is occurring.

The key then to helping us understand these future events is to correctly understand the meaning and timing of them. To begin, we need to look at what is happening in each of them individually. Then we can put them together and look at them as a whole. In this way we can see how they fit together with each other and finally, we will begin to see how they align with the other end times prophecies found in the bible.

SEVEN (7) SEALS of Book - **Opened by Lamb**

Ch. 6, 7 & 8

In Chapter 5 (vs.1) John describes seeing a book being held in the right hand of God while he sits on his throne in heaven. He describes this book as being ***written within and on the backside, and sealed with seven seals.***

Throughout history seals have been used by kings and rulers to authenticate official letters and documents. They were typically made from wax or some other soft substance to which an impression of the author could be applied. This waxy material was melted onto the document once it was folded closed. The impression or seal of the author was then pressed into the soft material. In this way the origin and the authenticity of the document were known by the person(s) who received it. The seal also served to insure that the document had not been altered or changed by someone else as it was being delivered. A broken seal meant the document had already been opened.

Seals continue to be used today to authenticate documents such as birth certificates and marriage records. The difference being that ink is used now instead of wax. A Notary for example applies their seal to authenticate signatures on contracts and deeds to real property.

In our study we read that God declared the end from the beginning (Is. 46: 10). He also declares that he is Lord and changes not (Mal. 3: 6), and his plan will stand. Here in the Book of Revelation we read that God has written his plan down in a book. To ensure its authenticity and to prevent someone else (Satan) from trying to change it, he has sealed that book with 7 seals. John states that only the **Lamb of God (Jesus),** is capable of breaking the seals and opening the book. As each seal is broken, an action or event begins.

FIRST SEAL: **(White Horse) Rider carries a bow & crown. Sent forth to conquer**

SECOND SEAL: **(Red Horse) Rider given power to take peace so that they should kill one another. Carries a great sword.**

<u>THIRD SEAL:</u>(Black Horse) Rider carries a pair of balances. One measure of wheat and 3 measures of barley for a penny (famine). Commanded not to hurt the oil & wine.

<u>FOURTH SEAL:</u> (Pale Horse) Rider named death. Hell follows him. Given power over fourth part of world to kill with sword, hunger, death, and beasts of earth.

FIFTH SEAL: Souls of Martyrs under Alter revealed crying with loud voice asking, "how long before their deaths are avenged?" Given white robes and told to wait until remaining brothers (fellow servants) on earth are killed.

SIXTH SEAL: Great Earthquake, Sun Blackened, Moon turned Red, Stars of Heaven fall to earth. Vision of Fig Tree losing figs from strong wind. Heaven opens like a scroll (God revealed to all on earth) Every mountain and island moved out of its place.

Kings and inhabitants of earth try to hide in dens and rocks crying, "fall on us and hide us from the face of him that sits on the throne and from the wrath of the Lamb" *(6:17)* *For the great day of his wrath is come: and who shall be able to stand?*

Ch. 7 Four Angels standing on the four corners of the earth, holding the four winds of earth, commanded by another angel which descends from the east, not to hurt the earth, seas, or trees until Gods Servants are sealed on their foreheads. 144,000 (Jews) from the Tribes of Israel receive the seal.

A great multitude of Saints from the Great Tribulation, clothed in white robes and carrying palms, gathers around the Throne. Angels, Elders & Four Beasts all fall before the Throne and worship God.

SEVENTH SEAL: (Ch. 8) Silence in Heaven for half an hour.

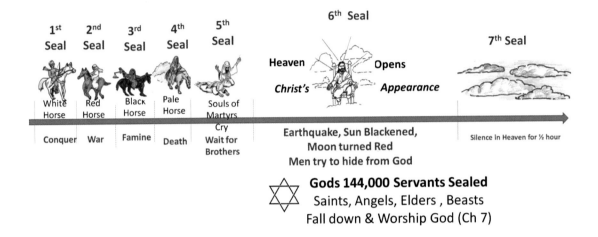

1st Seal	2nd Seal	3rd Seal	4th Seal	5th Seal	6th Seal	7th Seal
White Horse	Red Horse	Black Horse	Pale Horse	Souls of Martyrs Cry	Heaven Opens — Christ's Appearance	
Conquer	War	Famine	Death	Wait for Brothers	Earthquake, Sun Blackened, Moon turned Red / Men try to hide from God	Silence in Heaven for ½ hour

Gods 144,000 Servants Sealed
Saints, Angels, Elders , Beasts
Fall down & Worship God (Ch 7)

REVELATION 6, 7 & 8

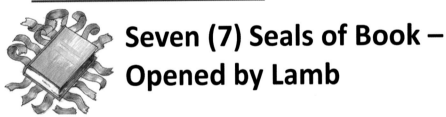

Seven (7) Seals of Book – Opened by Lamb

SEVEN TRUMPETS (3 Woes) - **Blown by Seven Angels**

Ch. 8, 9, 10 & 11   **which stand before God**

In Chapter 8 John describes seeing seven angels standing before God. Each of them being given a trumpet to blow.

Trumpets are used at social and political events to announce the formal entrance of someone important such as a dignitary. They are also used (blown) to announce the beginning of many events. In these passages we see that the purpose of each trumpet is to announce the beginning of a **judgment from God**.

The blowing of the first four trumpets announce judgments that affect the earth, sun, moon and stars. The judgments that follow the blowing of the last three trumpets however announce judgments directly against Satan and the remaining non believers on earth. John tells us that the judgments of these last 3 trumpets are so dreadful that after the blowing of the fourth trumpet , an angel is heard flying through heaven pronouncing **woe, woe, woe (one woe for each remaining trumpet)** on the inhabitants on the earth (8: 13).

It is important for us to remember that **it is not Gods desire that anyone should perish, but that all should come to eternal life.** That is the underlying reason that each of these judgments is delivered. By making a visible display of his power, God is attempting to reach out to the remaining unbelievers on earth. His hope is that they will be convinced to repent of their sins and turn to him. Sadly we read that even after the sixth trumpet is blown, those that had not yet died repented not from continuing to worship false idols, murdering, sorcery, fornication or thefts (9: 20 & 21).

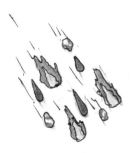

FIRST TRUMPET: Hail & Fire mingled with Blood cast upon earth. Burns a <u>third part</u> of the trees and <u>all</u> green grass.

SECOND TRUMPET: A Great Mountain burning with fire is cast into the sea. A <u>part</u> of the seas becomes blood, a <u>third part</u> of the creatures in the sea die, and a <u>third part</u> of the ships are destroyed.

THIRD TRUMPET: A Great Star named Wormwood falls from heaven onto a <u>third part</u> of the rivers and fountains of water, turning them to wormwood. Many men die from the bitter water.

FOURTH TRUMPET: A <u>third part</u> of the Sun, Moon and Stars are smitten. A <u>third part</u> of the day and night are darkened.

An Angel is heard flying through Heaven saying **Woe, Woe, Woe (3 Woes)** from the remaining trumpets to the inhabitants on earth.

FIFTH TRUMPET: A Star (Angel) falls from Heaven with the Key to the

(First Woe) Bottomless Pit (Abyss). Smoke from the pit darkens the sun and air as it is opened. **Locust with shapes like horses prepared for battle come out of the pit.** They wear golden crowns on their heads, have faces of men, hair of women, teeth of lions,k breastplates of iron, wings that sound like chariot horses running to battle, and tails like scorpions. They are commanded not to hurt the grass, trees, or any green thing on earth. Only men without the **Seal of God on their foreheads**. Not allowed to kill men, only <u>torment them with stings from their tails</u> for a period of 5 months. **The Angel of the Bottomless Pit who's name in Hebrew is Abaddon and Greek Apolyon (titles of Satan) is the king of the locust.**

SIXTH TRUMPET: Four Angels bound in Great River Euphrates set loose. They **(Second Woe)** have been prepared for an hour, a day, a month and a year to slay a third part of men. **They lead an army of horsemen numbering two hundred thousand thousand (200,000,000).** Riders have breastplates of fire, jacinth and brimstone. Horses have heads of lions which issue smoke and brimstone that kills a <u>third part</u> of men. Those not killed repented not from worship of idols, murdering, socery, fornication or thefts.

Ch. 10   Another Mighty Angel clothed with a cloud and rainbow upon his head, a face as the sun, and feet as pillars of fire, descends from heaven carrying a little book in his hand. He sets his right foot upon the sea, and his left foot on the earth and cries with a loud voice as when a lion roars. When he cries seven thunders utter their voices. John is commanded to seal up the words of these voices **(knowledge withheld).** The angel lifts his hand to heaven and swares by God and all of creation there <u>**should be time no longer.**</u> Foretells that the <u>**Mystery of God**</u> **as he has declared to his servants and prophets should be** <u>**finished when the Seventh Angel (trumpet) begins to sound.**</u>

Ch. 11   John is commanded to take the little book and eat it. It tastes sweet in his mouth and becomes bitter in his belly. He is then told to measure the Temple of God, and the Alter, and them that worship therein. Told that the Court of the Holy City (Jerusalem) is given to the gentiles to tread under foot for **3 ½ years.**

(Zach. 4: 2&3) The **Two Witnesses of God** appear and are given power to withhold rain, turn water into blood, and smite the earth with plagues. **Any man who attempts to hurt them will be killed. At the end of 3 ½ years when their prophesy is finished, the Beast that ascended out of the bottomless pit will slay the two witnesses. Their bodies remain in the street for 3 ½ days while the people rejoice over their deaths. At the end of 3 ½ days they rise up and ascend into heaven in a cloud. A great earthquake ensues knocking down a tenth part of the city and killing 7,000 men. The remaining people are scared and give glory to God.**

SEVENTH TRUMPET: A great voice in heaven announces that **"the kingdoms**

(Third Woe) **of the world have become the kingdoms of our Lord and his Christ".** The 24 Elders fall down and worship God. The dead are judged. Rewards are given to Gods Servants, Prophets, Saints, and those who fear his name. The destruction of those that destroyed the earth. The Temple of God in Heaven is opened to reveal the Ark of Gods Testament. Lightning's, voices, thundering, and earthquake and great hail proceed from the Temple.

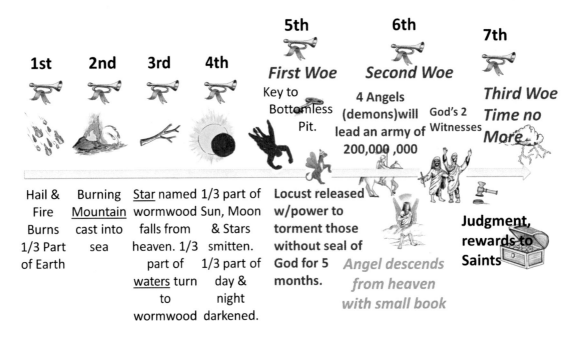

1st	2nd	3rd	4th	5th	6th	7th
				First Woe	**Second Woe**	**Third Woe Time no More**

Key to Bottomless Pit.

4 Angels (demons) will lead an army of 200,000,000

God's 2 Witnesses

| Hail & Fire Burns 1/3 Part of Earth | Burning Mountain cast into sea | Star named wormwood falls from heaven. 1/3 part of waters turn to wormwood | 1/3 part of Sun, Moon & Stars smitten. 1/3 part of day & night darkened. | Locust released w/power to torment those without seal of God for 5 months. | *Angel descends from heaven with small book* | Judgment, rewards to Saints |

REVELATION 8, 9, 10 & 11

 Seven Trumpets (3 Woes)
Blown by Seven Angels which stand before God

SEVEN BOWLS (VIALS) OF GODS WRATH (7 last plagues)

Poured out by Seven Angels from God's Temple

Ch. 15 & 16

In Chapters 15 & 16 we read of John's vision of the last 7 plagues from God. These plagues are described as being **full of the wrath of God** (15: 1).

Whereas the intent of the trumpet judgments was to try and bring unbelievers to repentance, here John is told that the plagues are delivered (poured out) as an expression of Gods anger. Seven angels are each given a vial or bowl (depending on your translation) containing a plague, and then commanded to pour them out upon the earth.

FIRST BOWEL: Poured on earth. Causes noisome and grievous sores on men with the **mark of the beast**, and those that worship his name.

SECOND BOWEL: Poured on sea causing it to turn to blood and killing everything in it.

THIRD BOWEL: Poured onto rivers and fountains of water causing them to turn to blood. Angel of waters proclaims Gods righteousness.

FOURTH BOWEL: Poured on the Sun causing it to **scorch** men with fire. Those scorched **blaspheme** the name of God **but refuse to repent.**

FIFTH BOWEL: Poured on the seat of the beast causing his kingdom to be **filled with darkness**. Men gnaw their tongues and **blaspheme God** because of their pains and sores, **but refuse to repent.**

SIXTH BOWEL: Poured onto Euphrates River, causing it to dry up so that the way for the Kings of the East might be prepared. Three unclean spirits like frogs come out of the mouths of the **Dragon, the Beast, and the False Prophet** (9 Spirits). These spirits go forth unto the kings of the whole world working miracles in order to gather them to battle at a place called **"Armageddon"**.

16:15 Behold I come as a thief. Blessed is he that watcheth and keepeth his garments, lest he walk naked and they see his shame.

SEVENTH BOWEL: Poured into air. **A great voice from the Throne in the Temple of Heaven declares "It is Done".**

There are voices, thunders, lightning's, and a great earthquake. The **Great City (Jerusalem)** is split into 3 parts. **The Cities of the Nations fall (Babylon),** the mountains and islands disappear. Great hail stone fall from heaven causing men to again **blaspheme God.**

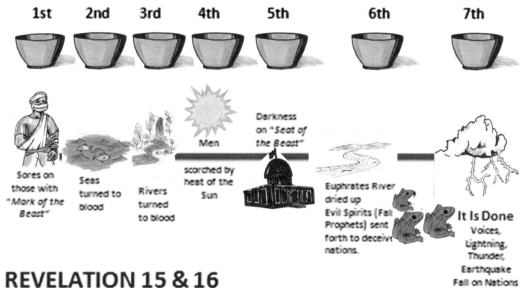

1st 2nd 3rd 4th 5th 6th 7th

Sores on those with *"Mark of the Beast"*

Seas turned to blood

Rivers turned to blood

Men scorched by heat of the Sun

Darkness on *"Seat of the Beast"*

Euphrates River dried up
Evil Spirits (False Prophets) sent forth to deceive nations.

It Is Done
Voices, Lightning, Thunder, Earthquake Fall on Nations

REVELATION 15 & 16

Seven Bowls of Gods Wrath

We have now listed all of the events that will occur during each of the the seal, trumpet and bowel events. If you followed closely as we read through them, you may have noticed there are some striking similarities in the descriptions of many of the events. Especially in those that are described in the trumpet judgments and bowel plagues. These similarities are no accident. They are in fact, one of the keys that will help us to understand these texts.

Before proceeding though let's step back and think one more time about these visions for a moment. As we discussed earlier, John was in exile on the isle of Patmos at the time he received them. He tells us that they occurred as he was *in the spirit on the Lord's day" (1:10)*. That would lead some to believe that he had been given the entire vision or book in one sitting. This is problematic though, even with the inspiration of the Holy Spirit it would have been difficult if not impossible for John to remember all the details he had just seen as he then sat down and started writing. It is more likely that the visions were broken in pieces and given over the course of several days, or even weeks. This would allow John time to sit down and accurately describe the numerous details and descriptions of what he had been shown.

Now imagine if you will, that you are at a football game and you are sitting on the 50 yard line. As you watched a play unfold on the field, you would probably not be able to see everything that happened on the far sideline. Likewise, if you were sitting in the end zone, you would not see everything that was happening on the opposite side of the line. Your vision would also be different if you watch the play from the opposite side of the field. So, even though you had watched the same play, you would see different details of it from each of the 3 different seats. So it was with John, as he was given the visions of the seals, trumpets and vials. He was watching the same events but, from a different spot each time. Notice how each vision begins with " And I saw." This serves to explain why some of the events (ie. Seas and rivers turning to blood, scorching sun burns earth, earthquakes, darkness, etc.) repeat in all three visions.

Now that we understand this, we can move forward and begin to piece all of the events together.. As we do so, a clearer picture of those end times will begin to emerge. Just as important, we will also see how these fit together with other prophetic passages in the bible.

Let's begin with the seven seals. The first four seals are most commonly referred to as the **Horsemen of the Apocalypse.** That title in fact is deceiving. If you look at their descriptions and those of the martyrs cries (5th seal), you can see that they match events that Jesus tells us are to occur <u>before</u> his return (Mt. 24: 5-12). These events in fact serve to prepare the way for Jesus to return. It is therefore reasonable to assume that these events occur in the period known as the Present or Church Age. That being said, many believe that these seals have already been broken and the events they describe are now happening.

When the 6ᵗʰ seal is broken we read that the heavens will roll back like a scroll, and God (Jesus) will <u>appear in the heavens</u> to everyone on earth. Many interpret this as him returning as the Messiah but, we are clearly told that his appearance here is heavenly. One of the primary roles of the Messiah when he returns is to liberate his people. That role is not fulfilled by Jesus until he physically returns with the armies of heaven to defend his chosen people the Jews. The event that occurs here therefore has to be the **Rapture** that 1 Thessalonians 4: 13-17 says occurs in the heavens. Depending on your position, we know that the rapture occurs before, during, or at the end of the Tribulation Period. The breaking of the sixth seal occurs during the Tribulation. The events described by it, including the rapture will occur at some point in that period.

In the first verse of Chapter 8 we read that when the seventh seal is broken, there is to be silence in heaven for a period of half an hour. For a long time the meaning and significance of this passage was lost to me. I struggled to understand what is occurring here. Then, one Sunday as I was listening to a sermon about worship, God allowed everything to fall into place for me. The pastor spoke about the need to revere God and be silent before him. For many, silence implies that nothing is or has occurred. If however we are continually talking, how will we hear what God has to say to us? Several things happen when we become quiet. Not only does our metabolism slow down, but our senses become more acute to what is happening around us. More importantly the clutter and activity of our minds fades away so that we can clearly hear and focus on what is being said to us. It is important for us to be quiet before God, so that we can hear what he has to say to us. That was it, that is what is occurring here as the seventh seal is broken. All of heaven becomes quiet so that Gods people can hear and understand what he has to say.

Because verse 8:2 proceeds to describe seven angels that are given seven trumpets, many presume these happen after the opening of the seven seals. This however as we will see, is not the case. Remember my analogy of the different seats at the football game? The vision of the seven seals and the seven trumpets are separate visions. John has been given a new heavenly seat to view the events of the angels with the trumpets!

The first 3 words of verse 2 *"And I saw"* are important. These serve to mark the beginning of John's new vision. The first verse of Chapter 8 describing the breaking of the seventh seal would be better served as the last verse of Chapter 7. Here it would be easier to see that the vision of the seals was finished. Once we understand this we can move forward and lay the new events described by the seven trumpets out on our timeline.

As we previously discussed, the purpose of the trumpets are to announce Gods final judgments on a sinful world. They are his final attempt to reach out to the remaining unbelievers and convince them to seek repentance. They must therefore occur after the rapture and prior to Jesus physical return to earth as the Messiah (second coming). That places them in the Tribulation Period.

Notice that as each judgment is announced they become progressively more severe than the one they precede. The first four trumpets announce plagues on the earth and heavens. While these will certainly bring fear to those remaining on earth, it isn't until the fifth judgment occurs that we see Satan is allowed to begin physically tormenting mankind. This will continue into the sixth judgment were a third part of those who are left will be killed by Satan's army. Sadly we read in verses 20 & 21 of chapter 9 that the hearts of men will be so cold that they will refuse to repent and turn from their wicked ways. All this happens as the stage is set for the last great battle known as Armageddon.

That battle will occur as the seventh judgment is announced. We are told that when that happens the kingdoms of the world will fall and become the kingdoms of the Lord (11: 15). It is then that the ***"mystery of God will be finished (10: 7)."*** His plan to restore mankind will be complete and all will know and see him as the true Lord of Creation.

This leads us to the vision of the seven bowels or vials. We are told by John (15: 1) that these bowels contain the seven last plagues from God, which are filled with his wrath. Again we read that the plagues will become progressively more severe as each of the bowels is poured out.

As the sixth plague is poured out we read that Satan will gather his army together to battle God Almighty (16: 14) in a place known as Armageddon (16: 16). From this we see that like the judgment of the trumpets, the plagues of the bowels occur prior to the physical return of Jesus to earth. You may have also noticed that the events that occur as each bowel is poured closely mirror events described by the judgments of the trumpets. Again this is no coincidence, John is being shown the same events from a different position in heaven.

When the seventh bowel is poured out a great voice is heard from the throne in Gods temple announcing **"It is done" (16: 17).** This is the same voice of God that is heard in Ezekiel 39: 8 at the end of the battle of Armageddon. There the Lord God announces that, ***"it is done, this is the day whereof I have spoken."*** There is thunder and lightning in the heavens, and a great earthquake on earth. All the nations of the world fall and become the kingdoms of our Lord (Ps. 86: 9).

Clearly these events all conclude at the end of the seven year period Daniel foretells occurring in chapter 9 verse 27 of his book. This is the period we understand as the Tribulation. They mark the end of this current era and the beginning of a new one known as the Millennium. In it we will live and reign with Christ for a thousand years (Rev. 20: 4).

Revelation Timeline

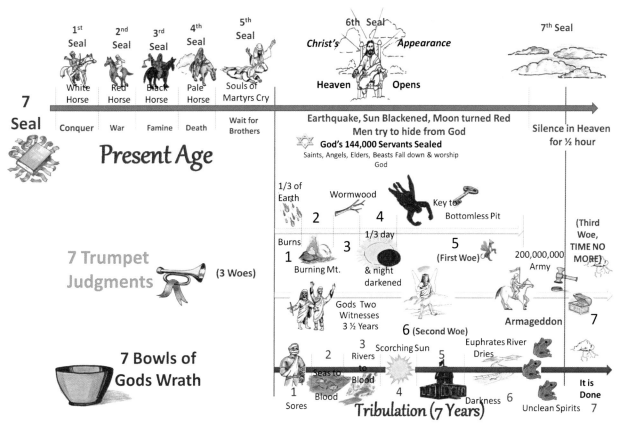

7 Seal

1st Seal — White Horse — Conquer
2nd Seal — Red Horse — War
3rd Seal — Black Horse — Famine
4th Seal — Pale Horse — Death
5th Seal — Souls of Martyrs Cry — Wait for Brothers

6th Seal — Christ's Appearance — Heaven Opens

7th Seal — Silence in Heaven for ½ hour

Present Age

Earthquake, Sun Blackened, Moon turned Red
Men try to hide from God
God's 144,000 Servants Sealed
Saints, Angels, Elders, Beasts Fall down & worship God

7 Trumpet Judgments (3 Woes)

1 — Burns — Burning Mt.
2 — 1/3 of Earth
3 — 1/3 day & night darkened
4 — Wormwood
5 — (First Woe)
Key to Bottomless Pit
Gods Two Witnesses 3 ½ Years
6 — (Second Woe)
200,000,000 Army — Armageddon
(Third Woe, TIME NO MORE)
7

7 Bowls of Gods Wrath

1 — Sores
2 — Seas to Blood
3 — Rivers to Blood
4 — Scorching Sun
5 — Darkness
Euphrates River Dries
6 — Unclean Spirits
7 — It is Done

Tribulation (7 Years)

47

WHAT ABOUT THE JEWS?

So, we have now taken a close look at the events that God has told us will take place before his return. If you are like me, you are probably also watching the things that are happening in the world now and wondering if these are the beginning of the signs Jesus spoke to us about in Mathew 24. Certainly we hear and see that there are wars and rumors of wars, nations continually strive against each other. There are famines, pestilence and earthquakes occurring throughout the world. As if these weren't enough, many Christian find that their beliefs and values are coming under increasing attack. As these erode we see the love of many waxing cold. All of these are certainly signs that Jesus told us to watch for.

Before we answer that question though, we need to look at one more prophesy from God. That is the prophesy concerning his chosen people the Jews (Ezekiel 37). Even though we are living in the Church Age, many people forget that the Jews are still Gods chosen people, and Israel is still his chosen nation (Deut. 7: 6 ; 14: 2). We "the gentiles" are the wild branch that has been grafted onto the olive tree (Rom. 17-32). We have been adopted into Gods family (Jn. 1: 12) and are now joint heirs of salvation through Jesus Christ (Eph. 3: 4-6, Gal. 3: 26-29). God has never forgotten the Jewish people. Even when they strayed away from him, he never forsook them. His desire was and continues to be that those who've strayed repent and return to him (Ezek. 18: 21-23).

Time and time again in the Old Testament God sent his prophets to warn the people when they strayed. After they did not repent, he sent other nations to conquer them. God knows that it is when we are at our weakest that we will turn to him and seek his help and direction in our lives. Remember the saying; there is no atheist in a fox hole! Though they did not know it, these conquering nations were serving as God's agents to humble his people. Those who didn't get killed in battle were often carried away captive, or forced to flee into other nations. Yet, each time this happened, a remnant of faithful Jews were always left behind to rebuild their fallen nation.

In the first two chapters of Malachi, the last book in the Old Testament, God recalls the covenants (promises) he made with the Jewish nation. Those were for them to be his people, and their priests to be their leaders. He goes on to remind them how they have systematically dishonored and rejected him by not following the conditions of these covenants.

The book of Malachi finishes with God's declaration that it is because of his love and the covenant he made with Jacob, that he will continue to honor them if they will return to him (3: 6&7) . Twice he promises that he will come to them, each time sending a messenger beforehand to prepare his way. Although not named in Malachi (3:1) Jesus would later tell us that the first messenger was John the Baptist. The second messenger we are told will be Elijah, (one of the two witnesses that will appear during the tribulation period) who will proceed Christ's second coming (4: 5&6). God also promises his people that when he does (physically) return to them, all nations will again call their nation blessed, and their land delightsome (3:12).

We mustn't forget that the Jewish nation has a very intrigull and important role in Gods plans both now, and in the end times. Satan also knows this, and is continually seeking ways to destroy them and thwart Gods plan. We are all familiar with the attempts he used during the Jewish holocaust of World War II. Despite Satan's continued attacks, the Jewish people have endured. They have in fact thrived in many of the nations that have welcomed them in.

On May 14th, 1945 what many believed impossible happened. The Jewish people retook their homeland, and the nation of Israel was reborn. This marked the fulfillment of several Old Testament prophesies concerning them and the approach of the end times (Jer. 23: 7&8, Mal. 3: 4, Isa. 10: 20-22 ; 11: 11&12: 43: 5&6, Ezek. 28: 25&26 ; 34:22 ; 36: 24). Probably the most profound of these is the vision that **Ezekiel** gives us in chapter **37**. This prophetic chapter describes the rebirth of the Jewish nation and the eventual return of <u>all</u> Jews to their homeland.

EZEKIEL 37

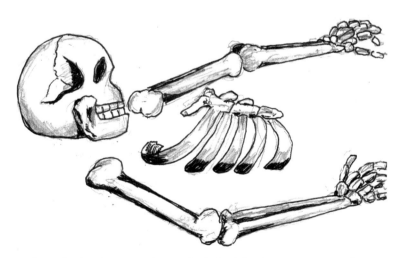

Vs. 11 *these bones are the <u>whole</u> house of Israel: behold, they say, Our bones are dried, and our hope is lost: we are cut off for our parts.*

Part 1 The State of the Jewish Nation & its People
Verses 1 -14

God had allowed the Jewish Nation to be destroyed and its people dispersed because of their continued rebellion and disobedience.

2 Kings 24 : 11 -16

Ezekiel 1 : 1

Malachi 2: 11, 3: 7

This condition had existed for a long period of time.

Vs. 2 Bones were many and <u>very dry</u>.

- None would believe the Jewish Nation could be restored.

Vs. 3 Can these bones live ?

- Through God's divine act, the People will be restored.

*Vs. 5 "Behold, I will cause <u>**breath**</u> to enter into you, and ye shall live:" breath "ruach" : soul/wind, spirit of God*

- The dispersed from around (four corners) the world made whole.

Vs. 9 … say to the wind, Thus saith the Lord God; Come from the four winds, O breath, and breathe upon these slain, that they may live.

- The resurrected return to the land of Israel.

Vs. 12 I will open your graves, and cause you to come up out of your graves, and bring you into the land of Israel

- All the people will know that God has restored them and placed them back in Israel.

Vs. 13 And <u>ye shall know that I am the Lord,</u> when I have opened your graves, O my people, and brought you up out of your graves,

Vs. 14 And shall put my spirit in you, and ye shall live, and I shall place you in your own land: <u>then shall ye know that I the Lord have spoken it, and performed it, saith the Lord.</u>

Part 2 Restoration (Revival) of Jewish Nation
Verses 15 - 23

One Nation, One King, A New Promise

- **The divided nation of Israel & Judah are to be rejoined.**

  Vs. 19 *…Thus saith the Lord God; Behold I will take the stick of Joseph, which is in the hand of Ephraim, and the tribes of Israel his fellows, and will put them with him, even with the stick of Judah, <u>and make them one stick, and they shall be one in mine hand.</u>*

  I Kings Chapters 11 & 12

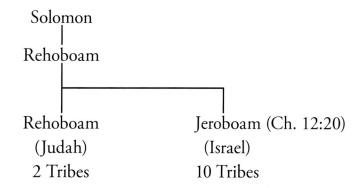

A single united nation with One King, <u>**One Shepherd.**</u>

  Vs. 24 <u>*And David my servant shall be king over them; and they all shall have* **one** **shepherd**</u>*; they shall also walk in my judgments, and observe my statutes, and do them.*

- David as the Shepherd & King, **an old testament type of Christ:**

    Ezekiel 34: 23 - 24

    Isaiah 9: 6&7

    Psalm 23: 1

- **God will establish a New Covenant of Peace.**

    Vs. 26 *Moreover I will make a covenant of peace with them; it shall be an everlasting covenant with them; I will place them, and multiply them, and will set my sanctuary in the midst of them for evermore.*

    Jeremiah 31: 31 - 34

    Ezekiel 34: 25

    Hebrews 9: 8 - 11

- **Gods relationship with his chosen people restored forevermore.**

    Vs. 27 …. *I will be their God, and they shall be my people.*

    II Samuel 7: 24

The prophesy of Ezekiel 37 was partially fulfilled when the Jewish nation was restored in 1948. Since then Jews from around the world have begun returning to their homeland. What remains is for the Jews to finally recognized Jesus as their God and Savior **"Yahweh"**. When this happens, his promise to be their King and shepherd will also be fulfilled.

So, when and how will this occur? As we've now seen, the entire world will be drawn to the Jewish home land as the end time approaches. The prophesies we've looked at will all culminate when the last great battle occurs at Armageddon. It is then that Jesus will return with the heavenly host to defeat Satan and those nations he has raised against the Jewish nation. It is then that every Jew will finally recognize Jesus as their long awaited Messiah.

The Gathering of the Nations
The Final Battle

So as we discussed way back in chapter 1, it doesn't matter if you are a Pre, Post or A Millenialist, we all agree on the sudden physical return of Jesus. In Revelation 19 he is described as returning on a white horse (vs. 11) leading the armies of heaven (vs. 14) to save his people. The Beast (Satan) waits with the kings of the earth and their armies to battle against him and the heavenly host (vs. 19). The vision of **Ezekiel (chapters 38 & 39)** written some 587 years before the birth of Christ, describes the details of this final battle.

We are told that the battle will take place in the Valley of Jehosophat (Joel 3: 2), or as it's known to Christians Armageddon (Rev. 16: 16). In the first six versus of Ezekiel we read that Satan's army will come down from the north out of the **land of Magog** against God's people.

For years western scholars have strongly believed that the "land of Magog" is a reference to the modern nation of Russia. Partly because Russia is not only geographically north of Israel, but the symbol of a bear has and continues to be used to describe their nation. It has thus been easy to assume that they must be the bear (second beast) that is described in Daniels dream (Dan. 7). We now know from our study though that the bear in Daniels dream is in fact the Medo Persian Empire.

At the time of Ezekiel's writing, the <u>nation of Magog existed in what is now modern Turkey</u>. **Meshech, Tubal and Gomer** were all city states of that nation. The ruler of the nation of Magag was named Gog, or Gugu (Greek Gygez). The Greeks referred to him as "Tyrannous" or "the Tyrant One".

One final clue we can use to understand where this nation that will be led by the beast will come from can be found in **Revelation chapter 2, verse 13.** Here God says to the Angel of the Church in Pergamos, " *I know thy works, and where thou dwelest, even where Satan's seat is"*. The seven Church's that God writes to here were all located in Asia Minor which is now modern Turkey. It is correct for us to assume that this will be the location of the land of Magog that Ezekiel reference in his prophecy.

EZEKIEL 38

Verses 1 – 6 Nations of the Antichrist/Satan

Gog (Rosh) : *Proper Name; Chief Prince of Meshech & Tubal*

Gog or Gugu (Grk Gygez) was the King of Lydia (part of Turkey) at the time of Ezekiel's writing. Gygez was known to the Greeks as "Tyrant" and the one who introduced "Tyranny". The Greeks called him "Tyrannous" or the Tyrant One. Like other places in the bible were God refers to the Antichrist as the Prince of Tyre, or the King of Babylon, or the Assyrian, He is calling the Antichrist "Gog" a reference to Gygez a real historic figure from Lydia (Turkey)

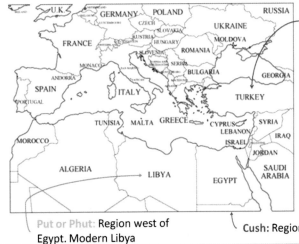

Nation of Magog: Lands of Asia Minor (Turkey)worshipped "Men" the moon god who's symbol is the crescent moon

Meshech: Located near what was known as Phrgia in central & western Asia Minor (Turkey)

Tubal: Located in Eastern Asia Minor (Turkey)

Gomer: Located in Central Turkey. Known to ancient world as Gimarrai of north central Asia Minor (Cappadocia)

Togarmah or Tigarimmu: A city state in eastern Anatolia (Asia Minor, Turkey). More specifically the southeastern part of Turkey near the Syrian Border.

Persia: Modern day Iran

Gen. 10: 2, I Chron. 1: 5, Isa. 66:19
Ez. 27: 13, 32: 26

Put or Phut: Region west of Egypt. Modern Libya

Cush: Region immediately south of Egypt. Modern Sudan, Somalia

- **Army will come from the north**
   Vs. 15 And thou shalt come from thy place out of the north parts, thou and many people with thee, all of them riding upon horses, a great company and a mighty army:
   *Rev. 2: 13a I know thy works, and where thou dwellest, **even where Satan's seat is:***
   Joel 3 … the valley of Jehosaphat   Rev. 16: 16 … Armageddon   Rev. 9: 17 Satan's army

EZEKIEL 38
The Gathering of the Nations - The Final Battle

NATION OF ISREAL

- **A warning for Gods people (Israel):**

  Vs. 7 Be thou prepared, and prepare for thyself, thou, and all thy company that are assembled unto thee and be thou a guard unto them.

  Vs. 8 After many days thou shalt be visited: in the latter years thou shalt come into the land that is <u>brought back from the sword</u>, and is <u>gathered out of many people,</u> against the mountains of Israel, which have been always waste; but it is brought forth out of the nations, and they shall dwell safely all of them.

- **Israel will be at peace:**

  Vs. 11 And thou shalt say, I will go up to the land of unwalled villages; I will go to them that are at rest, that dwell safely, all of them dwelling without walls and having neither bars nor gates.

- **Israel's will posses** great wealth**:**

  Vs. 12b …the people that are gathered out of the nations, which have gotten cattle and goods, that dwell in the midst of the land.

  Vs. 13b …to carry away silver and gold, to take away cattle and goods, to take a great spoil?

- <u>**Satan will use this wealth as the pretense for marching on Israel:**</u>

  Verses 11 - 13

<u>REMAINING NATIONS OF THE WORLD</u>

- **God will use the power of other world nations in the battle against Satan's army:**

    *Vs. 21 And I will call for a sword against him throughout **all my mountains (nations)** saith the Lord God: every man's sword shall be against his brother.*

    ***Ezekiel 28: 7** Behold therefore I will bring strangers upon thee, the **terrible (very powerful)** of the nations, and they shall draw their swords against the beauty of thy wisdom, and they shall defile thy brightness.*

GOD'S PURPOSE PROCLAIMED

    Vs 16…and I will bring thee against my land: <u>that the heathen may know me,</u> when I shall be sanctified in thee, O Gog, before their eyes.

    ***Vs. 23** Thus will I magnify myself, and sanctify myself, <u>and I will be known in the eyes of many nations, and they shall know that I am the Lord.</u>*

SATAN WILL PROVOKE GOD'S ANGER

    Vs. 18** And it shall come to pass at the same time when Gog shall come against the land of Israel, saith the Lord God, **that my fury shall come up in my face.

    ***Vs. 19** For in my jealousy and in the fire of my wrath have I spoken….*

THE WRATH OF GOD POURED OUT AGAINST THE ARMIES OF GOG

    Versus 19 - 22

- A great earthquake
- Fish , fowl, beasts, creeping things, and all men will shake at God's presence
- All Nations will fall
- Pestilence

- **Blood**

- **Hailstones, fire and brimstone rain down from heaven**

(7ᵗʰ Seal, Rev. 8: 5 ; 7ᵗʰ Trumpet (3ʳᵈ Woe), Rev. 11: 19 ; 7th Bowel, Rev. 16; 17 -21)

EZEKIEL 39
The Final Battle

- **SATAN'S DEFEAT:**

  Vs. 3 *And I will smite they bow out of thy left hand, and will cause thine arrows to fall out of thy right hand.*

  Vs. 5 *Thou shalt fall upon the open field: for I have spoken it, saith the Lord God.*

  Rev. 20: 1- 3 Satan is bound and cast into the bottomless pit for a thousand years.

EZEKIEL 39
"It is done"

- **The Destruction of Magog:**

  Vs. 6 *And I will send a fire on Magog, and among them that dwell carelessly in the isles: and they shall know that I am the Lord.*

  Vs. 8 "Behold, it is come, and <u>it is done,</u> saith the Lord God; this is the day whereof I have spoken."

  Revelation 16: 17 (7th bowel) *And the seventh angel poured out his vial into the air. And there came a great voice out of the temple of heaven, from the throne, saying,* **<u>It is done.</u>**

REVELATION 19
The Battle of Armageddon
Heavenly Events..........

Revelation 19: 11 – 16

The LORD of LORDS and KING of
KINGS will lead the Heavenly Host

- The **Beast** and **False Prophet** will be thrown into a lake of fire:

   Vs. 20 And the beast was taken and with him the false prophet that wrought miracles before him, with which he deceived them that had re3ceived the mark of the beast, and them that worshipped his image. These both were cast alive into a lake of fire burning with brimstone.

- The **Army of Satan** destroyed by God:

   Vs. 21 And the remnant were slain with the sword of him that sat upon the horse

- **Satan** bound and cast into the bottomless pit for a thousand years:
   Revelation 20: 1 - 3

- The Saints will be rewarded:

Vs. 4 *And I saw thrones, and they (saints) sat upon them, and judgment (bema - rewards/crowns) was given unto them: and I saw the souls of them that were beheaded for the witness of Jesus and for the word of God, and which had not worshipped the beast, neither his image, neither had received his mark upon their foreheads, or in their hands:*

Incorruptible Crown – **1 Cor. 9: 25**
Crown of Righteousness – **2 Tim. 4: 8**
Crown of Life – **James 1: 2**
Crown of Glory – **1 Peter 5: 4**
To Be Guarded – **Rev. 3: 11**

- **Saints** will live and reign with Christ for a thousand years:

    Vs. 4b *…and they lived and reigned with Christ a thousand years.*

    Vs. 6b *…but they shall be <u>priests of God</u> and of Christ, and shall reign with him a thousand years.*

THE FIRST RESURRECTION, BLESSED AND HOLY

Vs. 5 But the rest of the dead (those that have died apart from Christ) lived not again until the thousand years were finished, **_This is the first resurrection._**

Vs. 6a Blessed and holy is he that hath part in the first resurrection: on such **the second death hath no power,**

EZEKIEL 39
Meanwhile, back on Earth......

- Weapons of war will be destroyed:

  Vs. 9 & 19 Israel will gather and burn weapons for **7 years.**

- The birds and beasts will feast on the dead:

  Vs. 4b ...I will give thee unto the ravenous birds of every sort, and to the beasts of the field to be devoured.

  Vs. 17 - 20

  Rev. 19: 17 & 18

- The burying of the dead will take 7 months:
  Vs. 12 - 16 **_Full time work_**

THE WHOLE WORLD WILL ACKNOWLEDGE THE GLORY OF GOD

- The **Remnant** from the nations that came to assist Israel:

  Vs. 21 And I will set my glory among the **_heathen_**, *and all the* **_heathen_** *shall see my judgment that I have executed, and my hand that I have laid upon them.*

The **Nation of Israel**:

Vs. 28 *Then shall they know that I am the Lord their God, which caused them to be led into captivity among the heathen: but I have gathered them unto their own land, and have left none of them any more there.*

Vs. 29 Neither will I hide my face any more from them: for I have poured out my spirit upon the house of Israel, saith the Lord God.

WHAT'S NEXT ?

So, is this the end you expected? For those of us who have chosen to follow Jesus, it will only be the beginning. The beginning of a new life in which Jesus tells us that there will be no more tears, and no more sorrow. In Isaiah 45: 18 the God that formed the earth and made it tells us *"he created it not in vain, he formed it to be inhabited."* We are to live and dwell with our Lord and Savior forever on this world he created for us. The relationship that was lost with God when Adam and Eve ate the forbidden fruit will finally be restored, and Gods original plan for his creation will be fulfilled.

The knowledge of this, and what is to come can be both exciting and terrifying. Exciting, because of the hope that it brings to us as believers. Terrifying, because of the events that we now know must take place before we get to that point. As we saw, Daniel was given a vision of these events, and they <u>troubled him greatly.</u> So too we should be fearful of those things yet to come.

Do I see signs that we are nearing those end times? I would be naive if I didn't say yes but remember, Jesus told us that <u>no man</u> knows the hour or day in which he will return. Like our Lord and Savior, our desire then should be that no one should perish, but that all should come to a saving knowledge of him. I know I struggle with the thought that I may not get to see many of my family and friends again if they should die without knowing the Lord. Telling them this though can be difficult. That is one of the reasons I have written this book. Perhaps if they read and see what God has in store for this world, they will be convinced to follow him. I pray with all my heart that their minds will be opened, and their hearts will be softened.

Finally, we are commanded by Jesus to ***Love one another as he has loved us*** (**Jn. 15: 12**) . It is so easy for us to want to judge others, yet God tells us that we are to love those whom we might otherwise despise. This happens only as we open our heart and mind to God and begin to be transformed into his image. Through us the world will then see and know that Jesus is their only hope. May God's light shine through you.

In His Grace.

Printed in the United States
By Bookmasters